"This book will show you step-by-step how to deliberately create your greatest life. Master the steps and you'll live the life of your dreams."

—Denise Marek,
author of *CALM: A Proven Four-Step Process Designed Specifically for Women Who Worry*

"Simple, powerful and profound. Sonia takes a complex idea and makes the process of application in your experience simple!"

—Doreen Banaszak,
author of *Excuse Me, Your Life Is Now*

"This beautiful, clear and simple guide teaches you how to unleash and manifest your dreams. A definite must read book!"

—Carolyn Ellis,
author of *The 7 Pitfalls of Single Parenting: What to Avoid to Help Your Children Thrive after Divorce*

"Master all the steps in this book and you will achieve the life of your dreams!"

—Raymond Aaron,
New York Times Top Ten bestselling author of *Double Your Income Doing What You Love*

The Law
of Attraction
Plain and Simple

Create the Extraordinary Life That You Deserve

Sonia Ricotti

HAMPTON ROADS
PUBLISHING COMPANY, INC.

Cover design by The Book Designers
Cover art by © iStockphoto.com/chuwy
Interior artwork © iStockphoto.com/chuwy, jeremywebster,
LuisB, edge69, Palto, helloyiying, blamb, phi2

Hampton Roads Publishing Company, Inc.
PO Box 8107
Charlottesville, VA 22906

434-296-2772
fax: 434-296-5096
e-mail: hrpc@hrpub.com
www.hrpub.com

If you are unable to order this book from your local
bookseller, you may order directly from the publisher.
Call 434-296-2772.

Library of Congress Cataloging-in-Publication Data

Ricotti, Sonia, 1965-
 Law of attraction, plain and simple : create the extraordinary life that
you deserve / Sonia Ricotti.
     p. cm.
 Summary: "Eleven simple steps to attaining joy, freedom, and inner peace
in every area of life"--Provided by publisher.
 ISBN 978-1-57174-583-5 (5.5 x 6.5 tc : alk. paper)
1. New Thought. 2. Success. 3. Conduct of life. I. Title.
 BF639.R348 2008
 131--dc22
                                        2008019962
                          ISBN 978-1-57174-612-2
                          10 9 8 7 6 5 4 3 2 1
                  Printed on acid-free paper in the United States

This book is dedicated to my brother, Tony Ricotti. His infinite help, love, support, and positive energy have inspired me to realize all my dreams.

I also dedicate this book to my parents, Marlene and Roberto Ricotti, for their unconditional love and unwavering support throughout my life.

Contents

Preface

Mastering the steps presented in this book will lead you to live your greatest life.

Although today I am an author, speaker, trainer, and president of my own company, it wasn't always like that for me.

I spent most of my adult life trying to make a name for myself, attempting to become successful and create the life of my dreams. I eventually realized that what I thought was the life of my dreams wasn't what I dreamed at all. It was Western society's dream. I worked myself up that proverbial corporate ladder. I was proud of all my hard work and where it got me (several awards and a six-figure salary).

Yet, I felt like something was missing. I did experience a glimpse of true happiness on the few humanitarian

> **Sometimes we lose focus.**

missions I participated in around the world—I was living life in the zone during those times. However, once I was back to reality, the empty feeling would quickly resurface.

After much inner work and reflection, I realized that it was time to break free. I left my career, packed my bags, and decided to travel the world. I got a job as a tour leader for an adventure travel company and went from a six-figure salary to making twenty-five dollars a day.

The time away allowed me to regroup, reflect, and redirect my life. The experience was phenomenal. I realized that anything in life was possible.

At times we lose focus on what life is all about. We lose our true selves in the harried, crazy, busy lives we lead.

I decided to never go back to my "old" life; instead, I decided to dedicate my life to making a difference. I decided to create a transformational company called Lead Out Loud, which produces phenomenal leaders who live phenomenal lives all around the globe.

Leadership is a way of life. Leadership is a way of thinking,

> **"Leadership is a way of thinking."**

believing, acting, and inspiring. Anyone can be a leader. You can be a leader at home, at work, in the community, in the world, and, most importantly, within yourself.

UNLOCK THE DOOR TO YOUR GREATEST LIFE

To live your greatest life, you must first become a leader within yourself. Take charge of your life and begin attracting and manifesting all that you desire in life. Mastering the Law of Attraction is the key to unlocking the door to your greatest life.

A LETTER TO MYSELF

This "letter to myself" is a journal entry I wrote shortly after my return from traveling abroad for almost a year. I would like to share it with you, as I believe many people around the world are searching for positive transformational change in their lives.

JOURNAL ENTRY

This last year has been life-changing for me. We often crave change, but do not have either the courage, energy, or time to do it. All perfect excuses for doing nothing.

A big change occurred last year when I started to live life on my own terms, instead of someone else's terms. I now live life to the fullest and don't worry about what others think. I have determined what my values are and what I want most in life, and have aligned myself with those values and desires. Before last year I spent most of my time trying to look good or avoid looking bad as seen through the eyes of others. Why do we care? It is our lives, not theirs. I have come to terms with all that. I have actually embraced it. The more people laugh at me, the better it is. That means I am walking to the beat of my own drum—a drum no one else can relate to, but that's okay. I am who I want to be.

A year ago I decided to leave my six-figure income career to do a twenty-five-dollar-a-day job. In many ways it was insane, but it was the best thing I ever did. I worked on many projects that I was truly passionate about—I began writing a book, I launched a kindness movement, and I created a new business called Lead Out Loud—all while traveling the world. I met people from all walks of life and learned about many cultures. I experienced some very profound moments, moments I would never have experienced in my "old" life. So many experiences come to mind: my Christmas with the two young Mayan girls in Panajachel, the Mayan security guard and his memories of the 1994 Zapatista movement, and the people of Santiago de Atitlan after the mudslides. Cancun after the hurricane, the Teotihuacán spiritual experience, the vampire bat in the jungle, quiet reflections at Hierve de Agua, climbing the active Pacaya Volcano, and bathing in hot mineral springs. Oh, so many wonderful experiences.

How do I continue my chosen life? How do I ensure that I don't fall back into my old lifestyle? I can control how I live.

I Feel it. I Believe it. I Achieve it.

Life is short and sweet—make the best of it now. Love your loved ones, your friends, and strangers. I can make the world a better place. The world I choose is peaceful and loving.

I can decide what I want my legacy to be to the world and leave it behind. It is my choice. I can take action. Let's face it: I know I am on borrowed time. To Tim McGraw's song: Live life—like you were dying.

What a wonderful life it is.

—Sonia Ricotti

BELIEVE

"

To accomplish great things we must
not only act, but also dream;
not only plan, but also believe.

—Anatole France

"

Introduction

This book is about living your greatest life. It is about finding inner peace and happiness, and attracting and manifesting your dream life. It is about living the life you were born to live.

Living a great life is not easy to do. In order to attract your biggest and greatest life, you must master applying the Law of Attraction. Simply by understanding how this universal law works and mastering the steps presented in this book, you will ultimately attract into your life all that you desire.

This book will show you how to release all negative feelings and negative energy from your life. The goal is to get you to a place in your life where you are constantly in a positive state of mind, therefore constantly projecting positive energy. This positive energy will attract positive situations, people, and experiences into your life.

I have broken down this mastery process into eleven simple steps, explained in short, straightforward chapters. Each step is a huge one toward achieving inner peace, inner happiness, and a heightened level of enlightenment. This highly evolved state will attract and manifest itself into your greatest life!

WHAT WILL IT TAKE?

Mastering each step in this book is no easy task. It takes work, practice, and awareness. In fact, an entire book could be written on each step.

For our purposes, an overall understanding and awareness of each step will take you to the road to mastering the Law of Attraction. You will become the most positive person you know.

ENERGY

"

"The electromagnetic vibrations you send
out every split second of every day are
what have brought—and are continuing
to bring—everything into your life;
big or small, good or bad. Everything!"

—*Lynn Grabhorn*

"

The Law of Attraction

The Law of Attraction is a universal law that is present at all times. Put simply, it means like attracts like. The Law of Attraction states that thought energy and projected energy attract similar energy. As a result, we attract things into our lives according to our thoughts and projected energy. Simply stated, we attract into our lives whatever we direct our conscious attention to.

This universal law is an age-old principle that the world's greatest minds and teachers of the past have used without knowing its full scientific basis! Thankfully, we all have access to it through our increased understanding, and now almost all of today's most successful people are using it to make fundamental changes in their lives.

Our understanding of the Law of Attraction has been enhanced through our increased knowledge of quantum

"Like attracts like." physics. You don't need to comprehend all the intricate details of quantum physics to understand how this works. Every aspect of who we are—our bodies, our minds, our totality—is composed entirely of energy. This includes our thoughts! Everything that exists, from the dirt under your fingernails to the farthest star in the farthest galaxy, is composed of pure energy! This is not a theory—it is fact.

HOW DOES IT WORK?

The Law of Attraction is working at all times, regardless of your beliefs or your awareness of its presence. We are constantly attracting into our lives (whether deliberately or by default) what we are emitting into the universe.

What you focus on expands. Your thoughts are creating your reality. If you experience negative thoughts and feelings, you emit negative energy. You therefore attract negative events, people, and things into your life. If you experience positive thoughts and feelings, you emit positive energy. As a **"What you focus on expands."**

result, you will attract positive events, people, and things into your life. Understanding and properly applying this universal law is the key to achieving ultimate success in all areas of your life.

HOW TO APPLY THIS UNIVERSAL LAW

Fundamental to your using this knowledge to transform your life is understanding that you are applying this universal law even if you don't know it! You send either positive or negative energy into the universe. Like attracts like; whatever you are sending out to the universe will be returned to you. You are sending out energy right now, right this second.

What are you feeling right now? Are you feeling good, or are you feeling bad? If you are feeling good, you are sending out positive energy; if you are feeling bad, you are sending out negative energy. It is that simple.

If you want to live your greatest life, you must begin to do so by stopping the negative energy you project and instead emit positive energy—at all times.

Simply by shifting your thoughts, language, and, most important, emotions, you will successfully master this law. Keep in mind, this process is like using an undeveloped muscle—it takes time for it to become efficient and "second nature."

"You will master the Law of Attraction."

This eleven-step process will create the shift toward consciously and deliberately emitting positive energy at all times.

The
FIRST
Step

Decide What You Want

DECIDE

If you don't know where you are going,
you'll end up someplace else.

—*Yogi Berra*

Decide What You Want

What do you want? What do you really want? This is an important question to ponder. In order to truly manifest and attract all that you desire in life, you must first decide what you want. You must become clear on your vision of what your greatest life would look like.

Most people don't know what they want. Either they don't take the time to get clear about what they truly desire, or they focus on the things they don't want in life (for example, I don't want debt).

By focusing on the things you don't want, you are experiencing negative thoughts and therefore launching negative energy. This

"Become clear on your vision."

results in attracting more of the same negative situations, people, and experiences into your life.

Think about your thoughts. What do you usually think about? Are you complaining about what your life looks like right now? If so, chances are you are using negative language and focusing on the things you don't want in life. By doing so, you are only attracting more of the same into your life.

"Focus on what you want."

The key is to become clear about what you do want. Once you know what you do want and focus your attention on that, you will automatically project positive energy.

BE *UN*REALISTIC

When deciding what you want, be unrealistic. What would you want for yourself if anything was possible? This is a difficult task to accomplish for many people because they get stuck with "how" it will occur in their lives. If they don't know how that could ever possibly manifest itself in their lives, then they believe that it is not possible.

When I tell my coaching clients to dream big when deciding what they want, countless times they respond with, "But I have to be realistic." I always respond with, "Why?"

> **"Be unrealistic. Dream big."**

Be unrealistic. Dream big! Don't worry about exactly how what you want will develop in your life. Once you begin emitting powerful positive energy at all times, the universe will respond.

The only limits we have in our lives are the limits we impose on ourselves.

The "how" is unimportant; your job is to figure out the "what."

CREATE A LIST

One way of uncovering what you want in life is to make a list of all the things you don't want.

After you create this list, go through each and every statement and turn it into a positive statement of what you do want. For instance, if you say, "I don't want to have trouble paying the bills each month," you can turn that around to "Money comes easily and freely to me and bills are paid with ease."

Doing this exercise will force you to focus on the positive and also allows you to become clear about what you do want.

This is the first and most important step to truly achieving your greatest life. Once you discover what you truly want in life, then you can put your energy and focus on these things. By simply focusing on these positive things, you automatically generate positive thoughts and positive energy.

Tip

DECIDE WHAT YOU WANT

Write or type out the list of what you do want. Post it on your mirror, on your fridge, carry it around with you. This will be a constant reminder of what to focus on, where you are going, and what you will attract and manifest in your life.

What I Don't Want

1.
2.
3.
4.
5.
6.
7.
8.
9.
10.

What I Do Want

1.
2.
3.
4.
5.
6.
7.
8.
9.
10.

Decide What You Want

Choose Your Thoughts and Feelings

THOUGHTS

Nurture your mind with great thoughts, for you will never go any higher than you think.

—*Benjamin Disraeli*

Choose Your Thoughts and Feelings

D o you know that you can choose what you are thinking and feeling at all times? At first this may sound difficult to do, but by simply becoming aware of what you are
thinking and feeling, you can redirect negative thoughts
and feelings and turn them into positive thoughts and
feelings.

The best way to recognize a negative thought is to become
aware of how you are feeling. Anytime you are not feeling
good, you are thinking negative thoughts (whether you are
conscious of it or not) and therefore emitting negative energy.
Your feeling barometer will advise you on whether you are on
track to attracting and becoming all that you desire.

Right now, what does your feeling barometer read? On a scale from 1 to 10 (1 is feeling bad; 10 is feeling great), how good are you feeling

❝You can choose what you feel.❞

right now? The higher your level of feeling good, the more powerful positive energy you are emitting. Conversely, if you gave yourself a 2 out of 10 rating, the more powerful negative energy you are emitting.

By simply becoming aware of your feeling barometer, you can then consciously become aware of any negative feelings you are experiencing and then do what is necessary to change them.

Tip

CHOOSE YOUR THOUGHTS AND FEELINGS

On a piece of paper draw a big wheel with eight spokes representing these areas of your life: Finances, Health, Family/Friends, Romance/Significant Other, Career, Fun/Recreation, Personal Growth, and Service to Others. Then rate your satisfaction in each area on a scale from 1 to 10 (1 is closest to the hub of the wheel; 10 is at the outside). Which areas are most important to you? In which area would you like to increase your satisfaction? Write down what action it would take to reach the highest level of satisfaction (a 10).

So, for instance, if your feeling barometer is registering you at a level 2 in the financial area, what would it take to get you to a level 10? Perhaps you would like to make $100,000 this year. Write it down. This will allow you to visualize what a 10 would look like in that area of your life and help you focus on the end result of achieving that perfect 10.

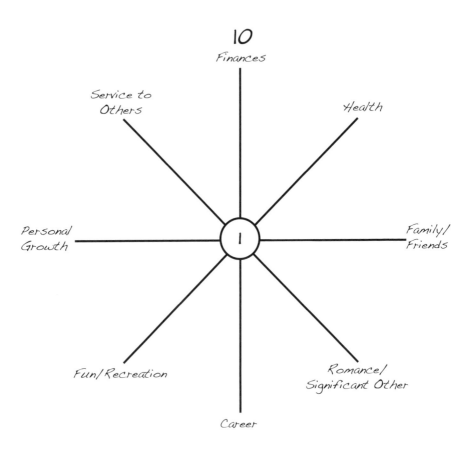

CHASE AWAY YOUR INNER SABOTEUR

We all have an inner saboteur. It is an inner voice that is telling you that you cannot do something, be someone, or have something. Recognize this as fear. It is normal to feel fear anytime you go outside your comfort zone. Anytime you do anything new and different, there is always some sort of inner voice telling you that you can't do it, that you aren't good enough, or that you may fail. Just recognize that the inner voice is you! The only person that is stopping you from living your greatest life is you!

"Recognize your inner saboteur."

Choose Your Thoughts and Feelings

Tip

Chase Away Your Inner Saboteur

Become aware of your inner saboteur. By simply being aware and recognizing when your saboteur is taking over, you can then take charge and slam the door on this unwelcome visitor.

Give your saboteur a name:

_____

Become aware and conscious of what your saboteur often tells you. So, when it shows up unexpectedly at the doorstep of your mind, you will immediately recognize it!

My saboteur often says:

_____

_____

_____

_____

_____

The
THIRD
Step

Keep the
End in Mind

START NOW

Though no one can go back and make a brand new start, anyone can start from now and make a brand new ending.

—*Anonymous*

Keep the End in Mind

At the end of your life, what do you want to be remembered for? What words and actions would describe your greatest self? This is an important question to ponder. If you were to pass away today, what would you want to be said about you at your memorial service?

It is important to take the time to reflect and determine whether you are truly living your greatest life or whether you have fallen into what I call the "treadmill trap." You're running and running and running fast, with no destination in mind, and arriving nowhere quickly.

"Begin with the end in mind."

Many people discover with this exercise that they are not at all what they would want to be if this were the last day of their lives. If this is the case with you, it is time to reevaluate how you are living your life.

LIVE BY YOUR VALUES AND WITH PURPOSE

Begin with the end in mind. At the end of your life, what *do* you want people to say about you? This will determine what your most important values are in your life. This will guide you to discover your true purpose on this Earth.

For instance, if you would want people to say something like "Samantha was a caring and loving mother and wife . . . ," then obviously family is one of your core values.

If you are currently unhappy with certain aspects of your life, chances are the way you are now living your life is not in alignment with your values.

Using the above example, if family is one of your values, yet you have been spending twelve-hour days at the office and traveling all the

"Align yourself with your values."

time, you are not living in alignment with your value of family.

Whenever you are not living in alignment with your values, the result is always dissatisfaction in that area of your life. This dissatisfaction is obviously generating negative feelings, which emit negative energy, which results in attracting more dissatisfaction into your life.

Being aware of your core values and then deliberately living and creating your life around those values will generate inner peace, freedom, happiness, and a life lived with purpose.

Tip

KEEP THE END IN MIND

Write out your eulogy. What do you want to be remembered for when you pass away? This eulogy will determine your core values.

What are your core values? Write them down. For examples of core values, see the appendix. Now evaluate how you are living your life. Is the way you are living your life in alignment with these values? If not, what changes do you need to make to ensure you are living your life in alignment with your core values?

It is imperative that you align your life with your core values in order to generate the positive energy required to attract all that you desire in life.

THE LAW OF ATTRACTION, PLAIN AND SIMPLE

VALUES WORKSHEET

Value/Description	Current Level of Satisfaction (scale from 1 to 10) 1 = low, 10 = high	Action to Be Taken to Increase Score (What would a "10" look like in this area?)

Keep the End in Mind

The
FOURTH
Step

Remove
Meaning

MEANING

"

Nothing is, unless our thinking makes it so.

—*William Shakespeare*

"

Remove Meaning

Do you know that we create the meaning of everything we experience in life? We decide whether an experience is positive, negative, or neutral. Many people believe that the meaning they give to their life experiences is real. The truth is that we choose how we interpret whatever we experience in life. Your interpretation of life events is based on your past experiences, beliefs, and upbringing. Realize that your interpretation of the situation is something you have made up. It is all a creation of your mind. You actually have the power to choose what feelings you attach to each situation, event, and experience. If you are not feeling good about something that has happened, think and reflect what interpretation you have given to that event.

For instance, if you were just let go from your job, and you are really upset about it, ask yourself, "Why am I feeling this way?" Your answer may be, "I can't believe my employer fired me. I worked so hard for ten years for them, and this is how they treat me. They don't appreciate me. They never appreciated me." In this scenario, you have made losing your job mean that your employer doesn't care about you and that you are not appreciated by them. Your interpretation of this situation can come from many different realms. It could be that in the past you were ignored by family members and were told you would amount to nothing; this could be the reason you interpret the situation in this specific way.

"You choose negative, positive, or neutral."

On the other hand, if you had a very loving, caring family environment growing up and were always told how wonderful you are, you could react to this situation differently. It may mean nothing personal to you, and you may say, "Oh well, what can you do? These things happen. Now I can look for my next, even better job opportunity."

These are two different interpretations attached to the same situation. Since we are the masters of interpreting all of our experiences, why not choose to interpret every single experience as positive? Since we are going to make up a meaning around the situation anyway, it may as well be some interpretation that makes us feel good. Every cloud has a silver lining.

The easiest way to do this is to separate the facts of the situation from your interpretation of the situation. The facts in the above example are: You worked for a company for ten years. You were let go from your position at this company. Those are the facts. That's it. Everything else is your interpretation. When you are conscious of this, you can choose your own positive meaning to attach to that event. You know you can even choose to make it mean nothing at all, to just let it go and move on.

It is important to recognize the difference between the facts of what happened and your interpretation of what happened. The sooner you are able to do that, the sooner you can begin consciously choosing interpretations that are positive in nature. These positive choices will keep you in a positive energy field no matter what the circumstances.

Remove Meaning

NOW, REREAD YOUR STORY
AND ANSWER THESE QUESTIONS:

1. Write out the *facts* of what happened (not your interpretation).

_____

_____

_____

_____

_____

_____

THE LAW OF ATTRACTION, PLAIN AND SIMPLE

2. Now, write out your *interpretation* of the situation.

_____

_____

_____

_____

_____

_____

_____

3. Turn that negative interpretation into a positive interpretation in that situation. Feel the positive energy
   flowing through you as you release that unwanted
   negative scenario.

_____

_____

_____

_____

_____

Remove Meaning

The
FIFTH
Step

Let Go

LETTING GO

When one door of happiness closes,
another opens; but often we look so
long at the closed door that we do not
see the one which has been opened for us.

—*Helen Keller*

Let Go

Let go. Let everything that is currently happening in your life "be." Accept your life exactly the way it is and exactly the way it isn't.

Accepting your life exactly the way it is doesn't mean you are resigning yourself to "this is how it will always be" and just giving up. That is not what letting go means.

STOP RESISTING

Stop resisting your life. Whenever you are feeling uncomfortable, unhappy, or any other negative emotion, you are resisting something in your life. You are saying to yourself and the universe that something is not right here and that

"Resisting is futile."

---

it should be another way. Resisting is futile because it does not change the situation. Resisting emits negative energy and attracts more of the same negative situations into your life.

You have two choices here. You can resist what is going on in your life and continue feeling unhappy, frustrated, and upset, or you can let go and accept it. By simply accepting

STOP RESISTING

What are you resisting in your life right now?

your life exactly the way it is and letting go of the way you think it should be, you are letting go of all resistance. You are freeing yourself from your negative emotions.

LIVING IN THE WORLD OF "SHOULDS"

How often do you use the word "should"? Anytime you are using the word to describe how things "should" be in your life, or how a situation "should" be, or how a person "should" act or behave, you are resisting what is. Be aware that this is generating negative energy.

RELEASE CONTROL

Many people have a tendency to try to control everything in their lives. In fact, anytime you are feeling resistance, it is actually a sign that you are trying to control a situation or a person. Recognize the fact that the only thing you have true control over is yourself. That's it.

WHAT YOU RESIST PERSISTS

When you refuse to let go and insist on resisting what is going on in your life, you are merely attracting more of the same into your life.

Recognize that anytime you are feeling a negative emotion, you are resisting something. Uncover what you are resisting, then let it just be **"Release and let go."** okay exactly the way it is. This release of resistance will automatically shift your negative energy to a positive one. Remember, as long as there is resistance in your life, you will continue to attract more of the same. Let go.

Accept the fact that "it is the way it is," and just let it all "be."

Tip

LET GO

The next time you are feeling uncomfortable, unhappy, or angry about a situation or person, ask yourself, "What am I resisting here?" Recognize you are trying to control an outcome. Then, release the resistance. Let it all be okay exactly the way it is and exactly the way it isn't.

For example, if you are $10,000 in debt, instead of constantly feeling bad about it, brooding over it, and stressing yourself out over it, which is resisting the situation (and, therefore, generating negative energy), simply accept the situation exactly the way it is. Accept it as a fact. Remove the meaning. It is not bad or good, it just "is." By doing that, you are releasing all the negative feelings and despair around this situation, and allowing the positive energy to flow back to you.

Let Go

The
SIXTH
Step

Forgive

FORGIVENESS

"

Forgiveness is freeing up and putting to better use the energy once consumed by holding grudges, harboring resentments, and nursing unhealed wounds. It is rediscovering the strengths we always had and relocating our limitless capacity to understand and accept other people and ourselves.

—*Sidney and Suzanne Simon*

"

Forgive

Forgiveness is the key to emitting and creating positive energy. Forgiveness is also one of the most difficult states to achieve.

We have all experienced negative events and situations in our lives. Many of us are holding grudges and resentment toward individuals for these events that happened.

By holding on to grudges, you are emitting self-defeating negative energy. Think about it. How does it feel when you think of that person? Do you feel good, or do you feel bad? If you are feeling bad, you are still harboring negative feelings toward that person or situation and therefore are emitting negative energy. It is equivalent to dragging around an anchor with you at all times.

In order to release that anchor and free yourself from these grudges and negative feelings that you are dragging around, you must let go of the feelings. How do you do that?

By forgiving. When you forgive, you are releasing that anchor.

Author Ann Lamott said it best:

> *"In fact, not forgiving is like drinking rat poison and then waiting for the rat to die."*

In reality, the only person dying is you. When you forgive someone, you are not doing it for the other person; you are doing it for yourself.

The simple act of forgiving automatically releases all the negative energy and feelings that were there for that person. Once you are able to forgive, you will feel a sense of inner peace and freedom, strengthening your positive energy field.

"Forgiving releases you."

BE THANKFUL FOR THE LEARNING EXPERIENCE

For every negative experience that enters our lives, there

is always something to learn and a way to grow from it. Identify the lesson learned. Recognize how you have grown from it and then be thankful for the experience. It is from our difficult experiences that we learn and grow the most. You can allow yourself to let go of the anger, resentment, and negative emotions that are attached to that individual or situation.

You are only hurting yourself by not forgiving. Stop resisting forgiveness. Forgive, and let go.

FORGIVE YOURSELF

Forgiving others is important to emitting positive energy, but forgiving yourself is just as important. Sometimes we hold grudges, anger, and resentment toward ourselves.

As we live our lives each day, we are learning. At times, we have made mistakes, been unkind, and behaved in a less than loving manner. We need to find the inner strength to forgive ourselves for our pasts. The past is who you once were, even if it was just moments ago; it is not

"The past is who you once were."

who you are now, or necessarily who you will become in the future.

You have the ability and freedom to start your new life, to be the person you know you truly choose to be.

Tip

FORGIVE

Think of a person you are having difficulty forgiving. Write out what you have learned and how you have grown from the situation that occurred.

Then, write a letter thanking that person for what happened. Explain what you learned and how you've grown as a person because of it. Then, forgive that person. Write: "I forgive you."

Note: The person you are writing to can also be someone who has passed away. You don't have to actually mail the letter or even speak to the person in order for the act of forgiveness to occur.

The
SEVENTH
Step

Unleash
the Past

THE PAST

> "
>
> Your past is not who you are,
> it's who you were.
>
> —*James Ray*
>
> "

Unleash the Past

M any people believe that the past is what has made us who we are today. And although I agree to a certain degree, that doesn't mean we must continually relive our past mistakes or regrets. By holding on to the negative feelings we have about our past, we limit our ability to become what we want to be, both today and in the future.

That doesn't mean we should pretend the past never happened; it just means we should leave the past where it belongs—in the past. Many of us take the negative feelings from our past experiences and bring them into our present and even into our future.

For example, if in a past relationship your partner cheated on you, that experience may affect future relationships. Each time you meet someone new, you may be apprehensive, be wary, or completely avoid getting serious altogether.

In this case, your negative painful experience of the past is affecting and essentially sabotaging all your present and your future relationships.

By releasing our attachment to the past, we create the open space of unlimited possibility and potential for the present and the future.

So in the above example, if you were to release that past experience and leave it in the past, you would be capable of entering a new relationship without preconditioned beliefs and thoughts. This leaves an open space to attract and manifest your dream relationship.

When I meet with my life coaching clients, one of the first questions I ask them is, "What does your dream life look like?" Once they have described their dream life, I follow with the question, "Why aren't you living your dream life today?" The reasons they give always revolve around the trials and tribulations they've experienced in life.

SO WHAT?

My next question is always, "So what?"

Now that may sound a little harsh, and I am definitely not discounting the experiences that life brings us. However, when we hold on to the past, all of our choices in life revolve around the past. By releasing the past and allowing it to just "be" and remain in the past, we can free ourselves to achieve anything we want in our lives.

Our negative experiences of the past create limiting beliefs and thoughts that are directing our present and future lives. Recognize that the only place the past resides is in our memories—in our minds. It is something we made up based on our interpretation of what happened. Although, we cannot change the past, we can change how we interpret the past and release our negative feelings, limiting beliefs, and thoughts.

The ultimate goal is to fashion an empty open space in front of you so you can create your dream life where anything is possible.

By holding on to negative past experiences, we generate negative energy. This inevitably will attract negative situations, people, and events into our lives. By freeing ourselves from the past, and giving up the hope that the past could have been different, we can then create a clearing in which to generate positive energy.

AWARENESS

Awareness is the first step toward leaving your past in the past. By simply being aware that you are holding on to the past, and recognizing the fact that most choices you make revolve around those experiences, you will automatically think twice and rethink your choice at that moment.

Author Robin Sharma said it best:

> *"Better awareness leads to better choices and better choices lead to better results."*

Tip

UNLEASH THE PAST

List the areas of your life that are affected by your past experiences.

_____

_____

_____

_____

How has your past affected the present status of each area? What are the limiting beliefs and thoughts that developed from those negative feelings surrounding your experiences?

_____

_____

_____

_____

Write down how each area would appear if you were to interpret those experiences in a different way and then consciously let go of those limiting beliefs and thoughts.

_____

_____

_____

_____

Unleash the Past

The
EIGHTH
Step

Be Grateful

GRATITUDE

66

Let us rise up and be thankful for if we didn't learn a lot today, at least we learned a little, and if we didn't learn a little, at least we didn't get sick, and if we got sick, at least we didn't die; so, let us all be thankful.

—Buddha

99

Be Grateful

The energy you put out to the universe is the same as the energy you receive from the universe. The step of being grateful for what you already have in your life is a phenomenal way to focus on the positive and emit positive energy. Simply by taking the time to focus on what you already have in your life, recognizing your great fortune and appreciating it will automatically put you in a "feel good" mood.

> **"Focus on what you already have."**

THE GRATITUDE MANIFESTO

Take the time to write out your own personal gratitude

Be Grateful

manifesto. This is a journal of all the things you are grateful for in your life. To get into that feeling of gratitude and appreciation, sit in silence, close your eyes, and begin visualizing everything you do have in your life.

Then write it all down.

Most of us spend much of our time focusing on things we don't want in life, discounting the marvelous things we do have in our lives.

Creating a personal gratitude manifesto allows you to appreciate what is already there and moves you into a positive energy mode.

"I am grateful for . . ."

Tip

BE GRATEFUL

Make it a habit to read your gratitude manifesto every day. Keep it on your nightstand next to your bed, and make it a habit to read it each and every morning upon awakening. This will begin your day on a "feel good" note, and your positive energy field will align itself to attract all that you desire for the rest of the day.

Choose Your Friends Carefully

FRIENDS

Keep away from people who try to belittle your ambition. Small people always do that, but the really great ones make you feel that you, too, can become great.

—*Mark Twain*

Choose Your
Friends Carefully

I remember when I was growing up my mother would always tell me:

> *"Tell me who your friends are, and I will tell you who you are."*

It is important to choose your friends carefully. Surround yourself with positive people.

You may be wondering, "How can I surround myself with positive people when most of the people out there are pretty miserable and negative?"

Do the people you surround yourself with elevate you? Do you walk away inspired, joyful, and full of positive energy? Or do you find yourself always giving advice, feeling mentally drained, and walking away with a black cloud over your head? People who frequently leave you in this depleted emotional state are energy drainers.

Stay away from those people. They will drain your positive energy and replace it with negative energy. Although you may not see energy, it is there, both negative and positive. Think about the times when you have met a person for the first time and thought, "I don't like this person. I feel negative vibes from him" or, "I really like this person. I get a really good vibe from her." That is all about energy the other person is radiating. You may not see it, but you feel it.

"Avoid negative people."

The same goes with the people you spend time with. Spend your time with positive people who generate positive energy. They are the ones who help elevate you to live your greatest life.

Spend time with people who are living the life you want to live. There are people living great lives. Who do you know that is living your dream life? Ask to meet with them, even if you don't personally know them. You will be surprised at how many people will say yes! By simply surrounding yourself with people who are positive, successful, and like-minded, you automatically feel good and increase the intensity of the energy field around you.

If you are having trouble finding people like that, then begin searching for workshops, organizations, and events that cater to the specific crowd you are interested in. For instance, my company Lead Out Loud (www.leadoutloud.com) hosts workshops and weekend retreats dedicated to mastering the Law of Attraction and living your greatest life. What better place to meet positive like-minded people!

CHOOSE YOUR FRIENDS CAREFULLY

Write down the names of all the people you would love to have lunch with, people who inspire you and positively influence you.

Pick up the phone, call them, and invite them for coffee or lunch.

Although some people may be busy, many will say yes. Most people will be flattered by your request. Who knows, they may even offer to mentor you.

The
TENTH
Step

Connect Mind, Body, and Spirit

HEALTH

Those who think they have no time
for bodily exercise will sooner or
later have to find time for illness.

—*Edward Stanley*

Connect Mind, Body, and Spirit

You hear people say this all the time: "I don't have time to exercise. I am too busy." The truth is we are all very busy in our lives. It is hard to juggle everything at once and fit all our responsibilities into each day. Our work and taking care of loved ones are our top priorities. We tend to put ourselves last. How can we be too busy to take care of the most important thing in our lives— ourselves?

"Exercise for yourself."

SET TIME ASIDE FOR YOU

Setting aside time for you each day is important. It is important for your mental well-being, your physical well-being, and your spiritual well-being. You will find that all the areas of your life are affected when you do not take time for yourself. Take the time to connect your mind, body, and spirit. It will connect and positively align you with the universe.

Tip

CLEAR ALL OBSTACLES

In order to set time aside for yourself each day, it is important to clear all obstacles in your way that may prevent you from practicing this very important daily Inner Champion Hour. Answer the following questions:

What are the obstacles in your life that have been preventing you from taking time for yourself and recharging your batteries?

How can you overcome those obstacles?

_____

_____

_____

_____

How will you, your family, and your life in general be positively affected by taking time each day for yourself?

_____

_____

_____

_____

Ensure you set aside time each day for yourself. A great time to do that is first thing in the morning before others are awake.

Connect Mind, Body, and Spirit

MEDITATION

Meditation is a phenomenal way to clear your mind, reduce stress, and achieve inner peace.

For some, it is an arduous task to sit still for thirty minutes and meditate. For some it is easy. It gets easier with practice.

If you are a beginner, guided meditation would be a great introduction to meditation. There are many guided meditation CDs and workshops to choose from.

EXERCISE

The benefits of exercise are both physical and mental. It not only increases your physical health and appearance, but it also reduces stress, increases mental clarity, and elevates self-esteem, to list only a few benefits.

Add an exercise program to your schedule. You don't have to exercise two hours a day, five days a week to reap the benefits of exercise. By setting aside twenty to thirty minutes, three times a week to exercise, you will begin reaping the benefits. Take a walk, join a health club, do yoga, or play tennis. It doesn't matter what you do. Do something that you enjoy. Just do something physical—anything.

WHOLESOME NUTRITION

You have probably heard the statement "you are what you eat." Nutrition is a key element to your overall physical and mental health.

Eating well-balanced meals and avoiding unhealthy foods will affect how you feel.

Think about the times when you ate a huge, heavy, fatty meal and how you felt afterward. You may have felt tired, lethargic, bloated, and unhealthy. All those feelings are negative. In order to feel good, choose healthy and wholesome foods.

NATURE

Being close to nature is a phenomenal way to create a feeling of connectedness and being at one with the universe.

Connect Mind, Body, and Spirit

Go for a hike in the forest, a walk on the beach, or a stroll in the park. Observe the birds, the trees, the flowers, and all of nature around you.

A DATE WITH YOURSELF

Each week go on a date with yourself. Schedule a day each week that you will just spend time with yourself. This time is "you" time; do something fun and different. Go to a movie, go to a museum, go to the park, go for a massage, do something you enjoy. This time is only for you.

JOURNAL

Journaling is essentially having a conversation with yourself. It is a great way to connect with your inner self and recognize and acknowledge what is going on in your life. The thoughts you write down will clearly determine whether you are emitting positive or negative energy. If your thoughts are positive, great, you are on the right track. If they are negative, recognize this red flag, and do what is necessary to release these unwelcome thoughts.

Tip

CONNECT MIND, BODY, AND SPIRIT

List examples of "mind" activities you can do and would enjoy—for example, reading poetry, visualization, meditation, journaling:

_____

_____

_____

_____

List examples of "body" activities you can do and would enjoy—for example, exercise, massage, yoga:

_____

_____

_____

_____

List examples of "spirit" activities you can do and would enjoy—for example, nature, journaling, meditation, music:

_____

_____

_____

_____

PLAN, PLAN, PLAN!

Setting aside time for you each day is important. It is as important, if not more important, than any other appointment or meeting you schedule in your day timer. Schedule your Inner Champion Hour in advance. Your Inner Champion Hour can be time you spend meditating, journaling, reading, or exercising. Take this

"Schedule your Inner Champion Hour."

time for yourself each day. It will rejuvenate and connect your mind, body, and spirit. Ultimately, it will place you in a positive energy field.

Sit down every Sunday evening and make your weekly schedule (massage appointment, meditation time, exercise, etc.). Include your Inner Champion Hour. What gets scheduled gets done.

Connect Mind, Body, and Spirit

The
ELEVENTH
and FINAL Step

Allow It

DOUBT

The only limit to our realization of tomorrow will be our doubts of today.

—*Franklin Roosevelt*

Allow It

By mastering the previous ten steps, you have arrived at the final step that will truly allow you to become one with the universe and attract and manifest into your life all that you desire.

This final step is to allow it to manifest in your life. Be prepared to receive it. In order to allow it to arrive, you must be free of any negative energy and have no doubt it will come to you.

"Have no doubt."

In essence, doubt is a negative emotion and emits a negative energy. In order to truly allow and receive all that you desire into your life, you must remove all doubt and believe it is coming to you. Only then will it materialize and manifest itself into your life. This can be achieved by three simple statements: feel it, believe it, achieve it.

FEEL IT

Feel like you already have what you want. This is important in order to truly release any doubt and negative energy.

Do what is necessary to truly feel what it would be like to already have it all. Deliberately focus on what you want with laser beam intensity.

"Focus with laser beam intensity." Go test drive your dream car. Go tour your dream home. Visualize in your mind and feel what it will be like with that perfect partner in your life.

Getting into that state of mind automatically generates excitement and positive feelings, bringing you closer to attracting all your goals.

BELIEVE IT

Believing you will attract all that you desire is important. If there is any doubt there, you are emitting negative energy. A great way to remove all doubt is to ask yourself is anyone out there doing what you want to do or has achieved what you want to achieve. If the answer is yes (and 99 percent of the time it is), then it is possible! If they are doing it or have achieved it, then so can you!

You must believe with every fiber of your being that you *will* achieve your greatest life.

ACHIEVE IT

Once you truly feel like you have already arrived at your greatest life and truly believe it will manifest itself in your life, there is only one thing that will happen . . . you will achieve it.

BECOME KEENLY AWARE!

Now, that doesn't mean that all you have to do is feel it, believe it, everything will just happen, and you will achieve it (although that does happen too). It means that the universe will align itself to send you the opportunities and events in your life that will take you there. You have to recognize and be aware of these signs and then take action. Don't ignore them. Don't think about it at length. Just take action. You may interpret these occurrences as coincidences, but it is really a sign that the universe is answering your request. Be present and aware when these opportunities arise.

Tip

ALLOW IT

In order to truly believe and release all doubt, create an attraction board or scrapbook. This is a beautiful visual tool to remind you of all the things and situations you will attract into your life. Simply cut and paste pictures of the things, people, and events you want to attract into your life. Keep it in a place where you can see it all the time as a constant reminder of what is to come into your life. All the pictures are snapshots of your future. This constant exposure will eventually nest into your subconscious mind, and the feeling of it manifesting itself in your life becomes real.

DREAM. DREAM BIG.

ANYTHING IS POSSIBLE
IF YOU BELIEVE!

Enjoy the Journey

LIVE LIFE

We are always getting ready
to live but never living.

—*Ralph Waldo Emerson*

Enjoy the Journey

The journey to living your greatest life and reaching a high level of enlightenment is not an easy one. It takes practice, awareness, and time to master.

As you apply and master the eleven steps in this book, you will realize and become keenly present to the true beauty of people and the overall beauty of life in general.

As you become more aware, peaceful, and appreciative, you will discover the incredible people, situations, and experiences that miraculously come into your life.

We must always keep our feet on the ground and never lose sight of who we truly are on the inside. Living a big life is not only about attracting great material things into your life, achieving phenomenal success in your career, or even attracting that perfect partner into your life. It is also about connecting with other human beings . . . it is about relationships.

By reaching this new level of enlightenment, you have the ability to make a difference in the lives of the people that you meet every day, be it family, friends, co-workers, or strangers. You can inspire others simply by being a phenomenal example of a great human being. Be uplifting to the people around you. That can take many forms: a compliment, a good deed, or even just a simple smile.

66

Leave each person you meet a little better than when you found them.

—Robin Sharma

99

Take the time to reflect, love, and enjoy every waking moment of this beautiful journey.
Peace.

SYMPTOMS OF INNER PEACE

A tendency to think and act spontaneously rather than acting on fears attached to past experience

An unmistakable ability to enjoy the moment

A loss of interest in judging other people

A loss of interest in judging self

A loss of interest in interpreting the actions of others

An inability to worry (this is a very serious symptom!)

Frequent overwhelming episodes of appreciation

Frequent acts of smiling

An increasing tendency to let things happen rather than to make them happen

An increased susceptibility to the love extended by others as well as the uncontrollable urge to extend it

—*Saskia Davis*

Enjoy the Journey

GET IN THE DRIVER'S SEAT

It is time to begin living your greatest life! The time is now! You have waited long enough; you must get in the driver's seat and finally get to where you want to go.

You now know exactly what you want. You are on the road to achieving inner peace and happiness. You are connecting mind, body, and spirit.

Now, you have come to the final stretch. You are almost there!

Here are twelve strategies that you can begin implementing right now. Don't wait for all the stars to line up to begin the journey, just begin now.

Tip

TWELVE STRATEGIES TO BEGIN IMPLEMENTING RIGHT NOW

1. LOVE YOURSELF

In order to truly live your greatest life, you must love yourself.

You must love yourself first before you can actually love others around you and project love out to the universe. Your are perfect exactly the way you are. Accept who you are. You have been put on this Earth to be exceptional.

Write a list of everything you love about yourself. (Perhaps you can add it to your gratitude manifesto so you are reminded all the time of how magnificent you are!)

2. LIVE IN THE MOMENT AND ENJOY THE JOURNEY

Celebrate and enjoy the journey, not just the destination. Just be. Think about it, all we have is the present. We need to enjoy the journey. So, savor every moment of your life. Celebrate simply being alive!

3. CREATE A MASTERMIND GROUP

A Mastermind Group is a group of anywhere from four to six people; a group of people who are creating phenomenal lives for themselves; a group of people who are looking to surround themselves with other phenomenal people to help and support each other to achieve all their dreams and goals.

Whom will you be inviting to be a member of your Mastermind Group?

4. FIND A MENTOR OR LIFE COACH (OR BOTH)

Who is living the life you want to live? Whom do you look up to? Whom can you learn from? Ask to meet with them. You'll be surprised how many people will take you under their wing and mentor you. Also, hiring a qualified life coach is a great way to keep you motivated, inspired, and on track to living your greatest life.

5. GROW, GROW, GROW

Never stop learning. Be open to new ideas, new philosophies, and new strategies. Read. Attend workshops/conferences. Watch inspirational movies (for example, movies from The Spiritual Cinema Circle).

6. EMBRACE THE FEAR

It is normal to feel fear anytime you go outside your comfort zone. Anytime you do anything new and different, there is always some sort of inner voice telling you that you can't do it, that you aren't good enough, or that you will fail. Just recognize that the inner voice is a saboteur! The saboteur is stopping you from living your greatest life!

7. WALK YOUR OWN PATH

In order to live your greatest life, you must be willing to do things differently. Do not follow the crowd. Be your true self. Be authentic. Don't worry or care about what others think. Some may laugh. So what? Many will follow. The only opinion that counts is your own.

8. CREATE AN ACTION PLAN

Create an action plan. Begin first with the final end result you want to achieve, and then work backward from there. The best way to create an action plan is to break it into segments of time.

Goal:

_____

To be achieved by what date?

_____

Now take a separate sheet of paper and begin planning what you want to do in time segments. So for instance, if you want to lose fifteen pounds in three months, you can break that down into monthly, weekly, and daily action plans.

Always celebrate your successes, even the small ones!

9. TAKE ACTION STEPS EVERY DAY

Start now. Not tomorrow, not next week, not next year, not when the kids are older, not when you have more money. Start now!

What is your plan? Put a solid plan of action together (daily, weekly, and monthly)—and implement it. As time goes on, be flexible. Don't be attached to the end result. You may be surprised that your path may take some unexpected turns as you go along. Go with the flow with ease. Your life may turn out even *better* than you expected!

10. NEVER GIVE UP

Never, ever, ever, give up. Many people give up just before they were about to turn the corner and achieve all their dreams.

> *Success seems to be largely a matter
> of HANGING ON after others have let go.*
>
> —*William Feather*

11. BE A LEADER AND ELEVATE OTHERS

We all have the ability to lead and inspire. Be a great role model. Elevate others around you to live their greatest lives!

12. TAKE THE LEAP

What are you waiting for? All we have is now. We all have dreams. We all have plans for what we would like to do in the future—"someday." The truth is, time flies. We get so busy with living our day-to-day hectic lives, that "someday" may never come. Just remember that when you are on your deathbed, you won't be regretting the things you did; you will be regretting the things you didn't do. Don't wait for all the stars to line up. Get out there and start living your greatest life!

If we wait for the moment when everything, absolutely everything is ready, we shall never begin.

—*Ivan Turgenev*

Enjoy the Journey

Creating World Peace and World Abundance

The awareness of this wonderful universal Law of Attraction is taking the world by storm. People all around the globe are deliberately applying it to their lives to attract all that they desire.

The question I have been pondering for quite a long while is, if it works for each of us on an individual level, what would happen if we all got together and focused on one thought together at the same time? How incredibly powerful that would be! Thousands of people focused and thinking of one positive thought. The energy would be off the charts.

The thought: creating world peace and world abundance.

As I am sure you noticed, the words I chose are positive in nature. I didn't say ending war and poverty. The words "war" and "poverty" are negative in nature. The more we talk about war, the more we attract it. The more we talk about poverty, the more we attract it. Mother Teresa understood this Law of Attraction when she said:

> *"I was once asked why I don't participate in anti-war demonstrations. I said that I will never do that, but as soon as you have a pro-peace rally, I'll be there."*

CREATE GLOBAL TRANSFORMATION

Each day we hear on the news how more and more people are killed in war. I do my best not to expose myself to such negative stimuli, as it affects my thoughts and feelings; however, I also feel that I cannot just sit quietly and pretend it isn't real.

I ask myself, how can we come together as a human race and create world peace?

I have traveled to many countries throughout the world on humanitarian missions. I have experienced firsthand the severe poverty that is rampant in many developing countries. I have witnessed with my own eyes children and adults with no fresh drinking water, barely enough food to survive, without any medical attention, and living in shacks that they call home.

It is a vision I cannot remove from my mind.

I ask myself, how can we come together as a human race and create world abundance?

HELP MAKE THIS DREAM A REALITY

Lead Out Loud is planning a series of exciting events to bring people together to focus on achieving this phenomenal goal using the Law of Attraction.

If you wish to be a part of this world peace and world abundance initiative, please go to www.leadoutloud.com. Go to the "contact us" link, and put your name on the "world abundance and world peace" mailing list.

Appendix

CORE VALUES

Abundance	Adventure
Acceptance	Affection
Accomplishment	Altruism
Accountability	Ambition
Accuracy	Appreciation
Achievement	Approachability
Acknowledgement	Assertiveness
Adaptability	Attentiveness
Advancement	Attractiveness

Authenticity	Confidence
Availability	Contentment
Awareness	Contribution
Balance	Control
Beauty	Conviction
Belonging	Cooperation
Benevolence	Courage
Bravery	Creativity
Calmness	Curiosity
Caring	Daring
Clarity	Decisiveness
Cleanliness	Dependability
Cleverness	Determination
Commitment	Devotion
Communication	Diligence
Community	Direction
Compassion	Discipline
Concentration	Diversity

Drive	Fairness
Education	Faith
Efficiency	Fame
Elegance	Family
Empathy	Fearlessness
Encouragement	Fidelity
Endurance	Financial Independence
Energy	Fitness
Enjoyment	Flexibility
Enlightenment	Focus
Entertainment	Forgiveness
Enthusiasm	Freedom
Equality	Friendship
Excellence	Fun
Excitement	Generosity
Exhilaration	Grace
Exploration	Gratitude
Expressiveness	Growth

Guidance	Joy
Happiness	Justice
Harmony	Kindness
Health	Knowledge
Honesty	Leadership
Humor	Learning
Imagination	Life Balance
Independence	Liveliness
Ingenuity	Love
Inner Peace	Loyalty
Inquisitiveness	Making a Difference
Insightfulness	Meticulousness
Inspiration	Modesty
Integrity	Motivation
Intelligence	Neatness
Intensity	Optimism
Intimacy	Organization
Intuition	Originality

Passion	Punctuality
Peace	Quietude
Perceptiveness	Recognition
Perfection	Recreation
Perseverance	Reflection
Persistence	Relaxation
Personal Growth	Reliability
Persuasiveness	Religiousness
Philanthropy	Resilience
Playfulness	Resourcefulness
Pleasure	Respect
Popularity	Responsibility
Power	Risk-taker
Precision	Romantic
Pride	Security
Privacy	Sensitivity
Professionalism	Serenity
Prosperity	Service

Simplicity

Sincerity

Solidarity

Solitude

Spirituality

Spontaneity

Stability

Strength

Structure

Success

Support

Teamwork

Tranquility

Truth

Understanding

Uniqueness

Vision

Vitality

Warmth

Wealth

Wellness

Wisdom

Acknowledgments

I would like to express my heartfelt appreciation to some very special people in my life:

Bill Wilson, for being my rock, my partner, and the person who elevates me every moment of every day.

Melinda Aszatlos, for her kindness and incredible graphic design abilities on all my projects.

Al Moscardelli, for being a great friend and business mentor.

Dr. Brad Deakin, my chiropractor and friend, for his encouragement, help, and efforts to keep me aligned with the universe with his phenomenal chiropractic care.

Danielle Joffe, my best friend, for her support and for always being there for me.

John St.Augustine, for believing in me, believing in this book, and extending a hand to make this dream a reality.

ABOUT LEAD OUT LOUD

Lead Out Loud is a transformational leadership and personal development company. Our purpose is to transform people around the globe into extraordinary individuals and create positive shifts worldwide.

Lead Out Loud offers a variety of products, such as books, audio books, audio seminars, inspirational videos, and downloads. Led by Sonia Ricotti, Lead Out Loud also offers seminars, workshops, retreats, coaching, keynote speeches, and various leadership programs.

As part of our desire to inspire and help transform people around the globe, Lead Out Loud offers a weekly radio talk show that focuses on motivational topics and conducts interviews with high-profile inspirational experts and role models. These shows are archived and available anytime for listening at no charge.

Lead Out Loud also offers a free newsletter. This popular motivating newsletter includes inspirational articles on personal and professional development and leadership, news on upcoming events, and tips on living your greatest life.

For more information on Lead Out Loud's products, radio talk show, monthly newsletter, and up-to-date events, visit www.leadoutloud.com. To inquire about Sonia Ricotti's availability to speak at your next event, contact us via email at info@leadoutloud.com or call 416.804.1974.

Acknowledgments

Sonia Ricotti is president of Lead Out Loud, a world-renowned transformational leadership and self-development firm that helps people achieve professional and personal success. She is a highly sought after motivational speaker, a leadership expert, a humanitarian, and a radio host for the popular inspirational Internet talk radio show, *Lead Out Loud Talk Radio.*

For more information, visit www.leadoutloud.com.

Hampton Roads Publishing Company

... for the evolving human spirit

HAMPTON ROADS PUBLISHING COMPANY publishes
books on a variety of subjects, including
spirituality, health, and other related topics.

For a copy of our latest trade catalog,
call 434-296-2772, or send your name and address to:

HAMPTON ROADS PUBLISHING COMPANY, INC.
PO BOX 8107 · CHARLOTTESVILLE, VA 22906
E-mail: hrpc@hrpub.com · www.hrpub.com